Astronaut
Life as a Scientist and Engineer in Space

by Ruth Owen

Consultant:

Kevin Yates
Fellow of the Royal Astronomical Society

Ruby Tuesday Books

Published in 2017 by Ruby Tuesday Books Ltd.

Editor: Mark J. Sachner
Designer: Emma Randall
Production: John Lingham

Photo Credits:
Alamy: Cover (top right), 4; ESA: Cover (bottom left), 10 (bottom), 12, 18, 22, 23 (top), 24, 28–29; Getty Images: 11, 13 (bottom), 17; NASA: Cover (top left), cover (bottom right), 5, 6–7, 8–9, 10 (top), 13 (top), 15, 16 (right), 19, 20–21, 23 (bottom), 25, 26–27; Science Photo Library: 14, 16 (left).

Library of Congress Control Number: 2016907601

ISBN 978-1-910549-87-2

Printed and published in the United States of America

For further information including rights and permissions requests, please contact our Customer Service Department at 877-337-8577.

Contents

Just Another Day at Work

The countdown is over. A deafening roar bursts from the base of the Soyuz-FG rocket. As people around the world hold their breath, the rocket soars into the sky on a column of flame.

Blasting away from Earth are Timothy Kopra, Yuri Malenchenko, and Tim Peake. Just three scientists and **engineers** on their way to work!

In a few hours, the men will reach their destination—the International Space Station (ISS). Their training has been long and hard. But it will all be worth it to have the chance to live and work high above Earth in the most extreme **laboratory** ever built!

ISS Expedition 46 crew members Tim Peake (left), Yuri Malenchenko (center), and Timothy Kopra (right) preflight, December 15, 2015.

Astronauts are highly skilled men and women. They may be scientists, engineers, pilots—or all three. Astronauts work for space agencies such as NASA (National Aeronautics and Space Administration) and ESA (European Space Agency).

The Soyuz-FG blasts off from the Baikonur Cosmodrome in Kazakhstan.

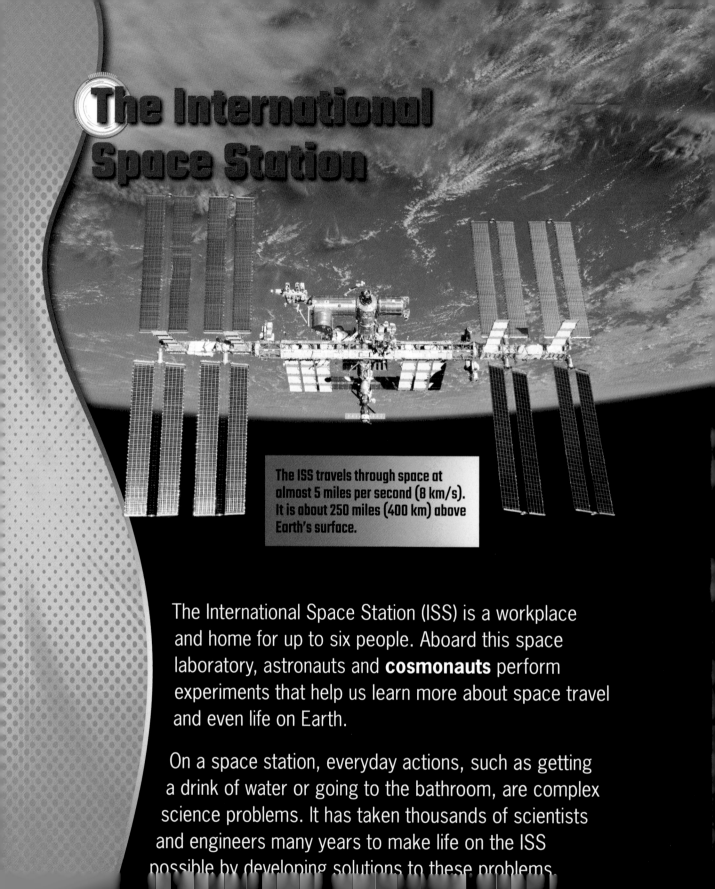

The International Space Station

The ISS travels through space at almost 5 miles per second (8 km/s). It is about 250 miles (400 km) above Earth's surface.

The International Space Station (ISS) is a workplace and home for up to six people. Aboard this space laboratory, astronauts and **cosmonauts** perform experiments that help us learn more about space travel and even life on Earth.

On a space station, everyday actions, such as getting a drink of water or going to the bathroom, are complex science problems. It has taken thousands of scientists and engineers many years to make life on the ISS possible by developing solutions to these problems.

Astronaut and engineer Karen Nyberg watches Earth from the ISS.
Watching their home planet is a favorite activity for the ISS crew.

The ISS **orbits** Earth 16 times in every 24-hour period. During each orbit, it moves into the Sun's light for 45 minutes and then into darkness for 45 minutes. This means the crew experiences 16 sunrises and 16 sunsets every day.

On Earth, **gravity** pulls everything, including us, down toward the ground. Inside the ISS or an orbiting spacecraft, everything experiences zero gravity and astronauts feel weightless.

Astronaut Training

Do you want to be an astronaut? When British pilot Tim Peake read the European Space Agency's (ESA's) advertisement, his answer was yes!

After beating more than 8,000 other applicants to get his dream job, Tim began six years of grueling astronaut training.

Astronauts on an ISS mission must learn every detail of how the space station works, and how to fix it if something goes wrong. A task that may take just one hour on the ISS will be practiced for hundreds of hours on Earth inside a **simulator**.

Tim Peake and Timothy Kopra in NASA's Systems Engineering Simulator at the Johnson Space Center, Houston.

The simulator can be programmed to recreate what astronauts will see and do on the ISS.

During training, Tim Peake and other astronauts spent six days underground in a cave. They practiced working as a team in this extreme environment.

Astronauts study and prepare for the science experiments they will do in space. They also undergo medical training. When you're 250 miles (400 km) above Earth, you can't call a doctor. So all astronaut trainees learn procedures, such as giving shots, stitching up wounds, and helping someone who has stopped breathing.

Winter survival training in Russia

If something goes wrong during its landing, a spacecraft may crash in a remote wilderness area. During survival training, astronauts prepare for this by making shelters, building fires, and even foraging for food in the wild.

Training for Zero Gravity

Time on the "Vomit Comet" is a must for every astronaut trainee!

To prepare for zero gravity in space, astronauts take training flights on a specially fitted aircraft. During a flight, the plane makes extreme climbs and dips. This creates zero gravity inside the plane for up to 25 seconds at a time. During the periods of weightlessness, astronauts practice moving around and doing tasks.

Reduced gravity plane

Samantha Cristoforetti practices using tools during a zero gravity flight.

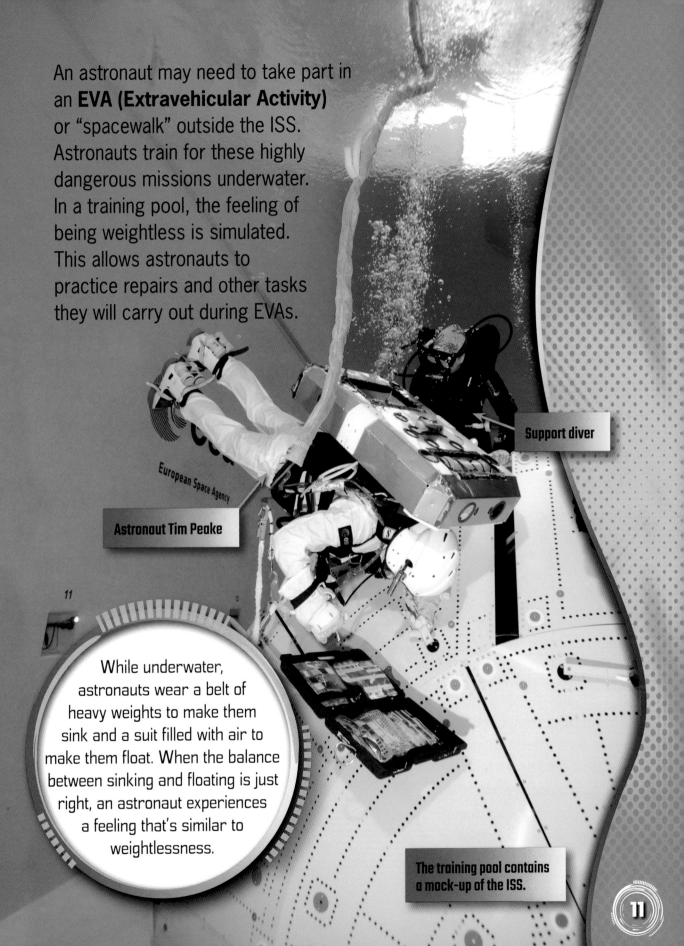

An astronaut may need to take part in an **EVA (Extravehicular Activity)** or "spacewalk" outside the ISS. Astronauts train for these highly dangerous missions underwater. In a training pool, the feeling of being weightless is simulated. This allows astronauts to practice repairs and other tasks they will carry out during EVAs.

European Space Agency

Astronaut Tim Peake

Support diver

While underwater, astronauts wear a belt of heavy weights to make them sink and a suit filled with air to make them float. When the balance between sinking and floating is just right, an astronaut experiences a feeling that's similar to weightlessness.

The training pool contains a mock-up of the ISS.

If the years of training are successful, an astronaut may one day be part of a crew hurtling away from Earth in a tiny *Soyuz* spacecraft.

A *Soyuz* spacecraft is a tight squeeze! Here, a crew is crammed into a mock-up craft during training.

As a theme park ride accelerates, you might be pushed back into your seat. The acceleration experienced by astronauts during a launch is a little like that—only it feels like a baby elephant is sitting on their lap!

A *Soyuz* spacecraft docked with the ISS

It can take as little as six hours for the spacecraft to reach the ISS. Once the craft has **docked**, and a long list of checks is complete, the crew boards the space station.

Now that they are aboard the ISS, astronauts will neither feel nor taste fresh air for many months. The space station's Elektron system uses water, such as waste water from washing, to create breathable **oxygen**. The system separates **water molecules** into oxygen and hydrogen. The oxygen is pumped into the station for breathing. The hydrogen is vented, or released, into space.

Astronaut Scott Kelly welcomes Tim Peake aboard the ISS.

Life on the Space Station

Aboard the ISS, water is precious. The crew uses as little as possible for washing up. They use "no rinse" shampoo that they simply comb through their hair. They also use edible toothpaste, so no water is wasted rinsing teeth.

All waste water on the ISS is recycled. Even the astronauts' urine is cleaned and recycled back into fresh drinking water.

Water is heavy, so it's not practical to send the water that astronauts need into space. Finding ways to recycle water aboard the ISS was a major challenge for the engineers and scientists who designed the space station.

In zero gravity, water and other liquids don't flow. Liquids form into floating globules, or bubbles.

Water globule

Astronauts use a straw to suck drinks and soups from a pouch.

Food aboard the ISS is specially developed to be long-lasting and crumb free. Crumbs might float away and **contaminate** equipment. Even salt and pepper are liquid. This stops tiny particles from clogging air vents or floating into an astronaut's eyes or nose.

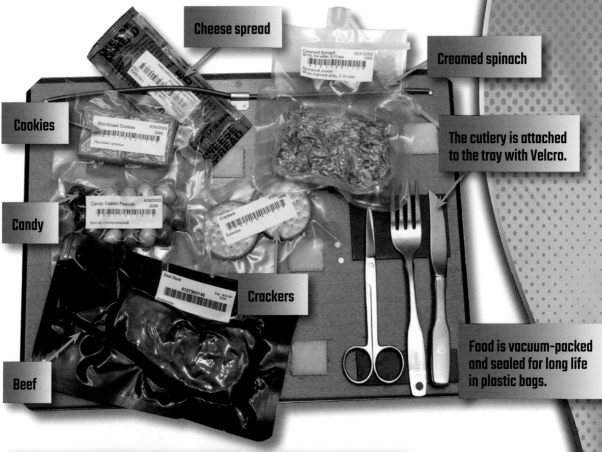

Cheese spread

Creamed spinach

Cookies

The cutlery is attached to the tray with Velcro.

Candy

Crackers

Food is vacuum-packed and sealed for long life in plastic bags.

Beef

When a supply spacecraft arrives from Earth, the ISS crew gets a delivery of fruit, vegetables, and other fresh foods.

Sleeping, Running, and . . .

On the ISS, astronauts have to be neat or the air would be full of floating food, tools, socks. . . . Astronauts even sleep in sleeping bags anchored to the walls of their crew cabins.

Weightlessness makes an astronaut's muscles and bones grow weak. To keep their bodies strong, astronauts work out for two hours every day on the station's treadmill, stationary bike, and resistance equipment.

Samantha Cristoforetti in her sleeping bag inside a tiny crew cabin.

Astronauts relax by watching movies and playing games. The chess pieces in this game are attached to the board by Velcro.

In April 2016, Tim Peake ran the London Marathon in zero gravity on the ISS. He was strapped to the treadmill by bungee cords.

And the really big question?

When going to the bathroom, astronauts pee into a funnel attached to a pipe. Air then sucks the liquid away so it cannot escape. When sitting on the toilet, astronauts use seatbelt-like straps so they don't float off!

On the ISS, urine is recycled into fresh water. For now, there is no use for other waste. A future scientific challenge is to find a way to recycle astronaut poop into something useful.

Astronaut Scientists at Work

Every day, the crew of the ISS works on science experiments in the space station's laboratories.

The astronauts study metals by melting and then rapidly cooling them. In zero gravity, metals behave differently than they do on Earth, because gravity is not pulling on them. The **data** collected in these experiments can be used to produce new types of metal that are stronger or lighter.

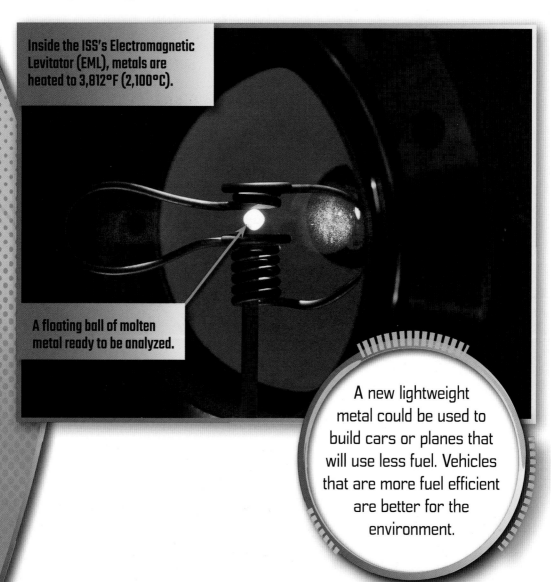

Inside the ISS's Electromagnetic Levitator (EML), metals are heated to 3,812°F (2,100°C).

A floating ball of molten metal ready to be analyzed.

A new lightweight metal could be used to build cars or planes that will use less fuel. Vehicles that are more fuel efficient are better for the environment.

This illustration shows how a spacecraft in the future might have an area for growing plants, such as beets, lettuce, tomatoes, zucchini, and beans.

In the future, humans may make long flights to Mars. Astronauts on these missions will have to grow their own food on their spacecraft.

Aboard the ISS, astronauts carry out experiments to learn how conditions such as zero gravity and **radiation** affect how plants grow. This research could help scientists develop new ways to grow "space-ready" varieties of vegetables and other new plants.

Astronauts Kjell Lindgren and Scott Kelly eat some lettuce that has been grown on the ISS in a system called the Veggie System.

A Human Experiment

A mission to Mars and back could last for two years. How will living in space for that long affect an astronaut's body? Astronaut Scott Kelly actually became a human experiment to help answer that question.

Before Scott went to the ISS, he underwent extensive medical tests and examinations. After 340 days on the ISS, he returned to Earth to undergo further testing and monitoring.

Scott's twin brother Mark was also tested and examined. Mark, however, did not go into space.

Now scientists will study the twins and compare them. They hope to learn in what ways the long stay in space has affected Scott's body and health.

Scott Kelly takes part in an experiment aboard the ISS to study how the body's fluids, such as blood, behave in zero gravity.

Scott (top, aboard the ISS) and Mark (below, on Earth) give themselves flu shots. Scientists will investigate if being in space changes Scott's ability to fight off illnesses.

During his mission, Scott monitored many parts of his body, including his eyes and heart. He also took samples from his body, such as blood, saliva, urine, and poop. The samples were stored safely on the ISS so they could be analyzed back on Earth.

Ready to Spacewalk

The ultimate experience for any astronaut is to take part in an EVA, or spacewalk.

During a spacewalk, an astronaut wears a spacesuit called an Extravehicular Mobility Unit (EMU). Like a one-person spacecraft, an EMU supplies the astronaut with oxygen to breathe and water to drink. It also contains radio equipment to allow the astronaut to communicate with an EVA partner and the crew members still inside the ISS.

The astronauts put on their EMUs in a tiny room called an airlock. Once they are ready, the door that leads back into the space station is tightly closed. This keeps the air inside the space station from escaping. Then the astronauts open the airlock's second door. This door leads out into the blackness of space.

Beneath the EMU, an astronaut wears a one-piece suit called a Liquid Cooling and Ventilation Garment. Tubes carry cold water through this suit to keep the astronaut cool. An astronaut also wears diaper-like underwear.

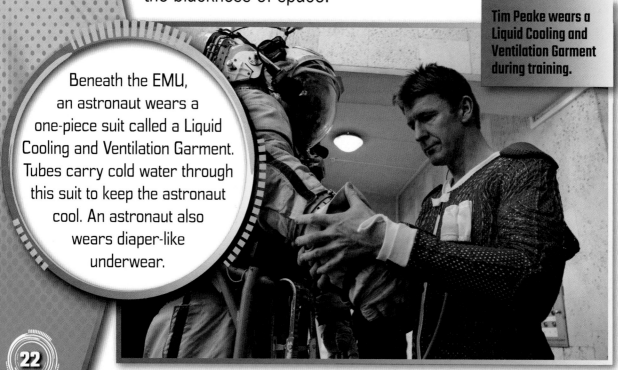

Tim Peake wears a Liquid Cooling and Ventilation Garment during training.

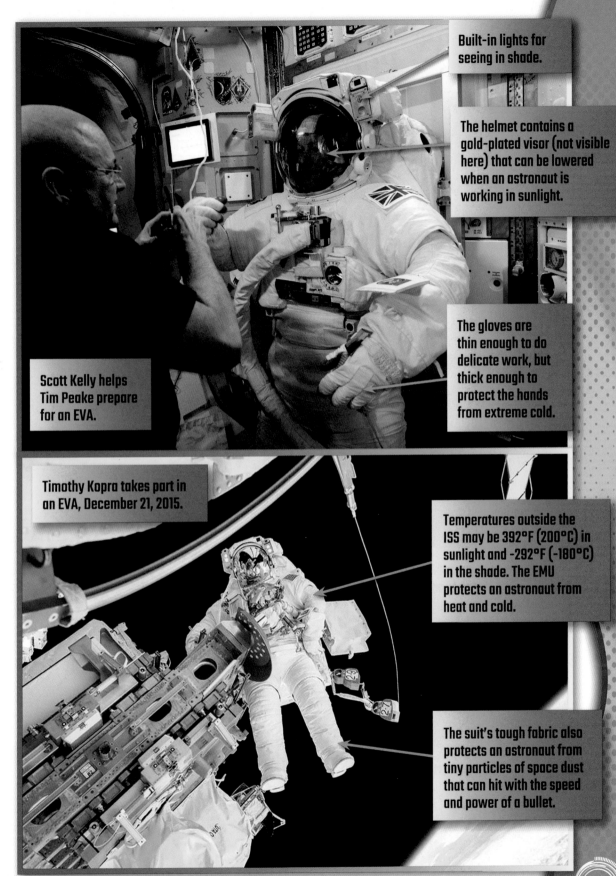

Built-in lights for seeing in shade.

The helmet contains a gold-plated visor (not visible here) that can be lowered when an astronaut is working in sunlight.

The gloves are thin enough to do delicate work, but thick enough to protect the hands from extreme cold.

Scott Kelly helps Tim Peake prepare for an EVA.

Timothy Kopra takes part in an EVA, December 21, 2015.

Temperatures outside the ISS may be 392°F (200°C) in sunlight and -292°F (-180°C) in the shade. The EMU protects an astronaut from heat and cold.

The suit's tough fabric also protects an astronaut from tiny particles of space dust that can hit with the speed and power of a bullet.

Walking in Space

On January 15, 2016, astronauts Timothy Kopra and Tim Peake performed an EVA. The purpose of their mission was to replace a box of electronics on one of the station's huge **solar arrays**.

The two astronauts climbed almost to the opposite end of the station to the airlock door. Once they were in position, they waited for the ISS to move into darkness. With Earth blocking the Sun's light, they had just 30 minutes to replace the power unit. Once the ISS flew back into sunlight, high voltage electricity would surge through the electronics.

Working with tools such as a wrench and a pistol-grip screwdriver, they successfully replaced the power unit. It was a simple engineering task, but it was performed under the most dangerous and extreme conditions!

Tim Peake working outside the ISS during his EVA. The spacewalk lasted for four hours and 43 minutes.

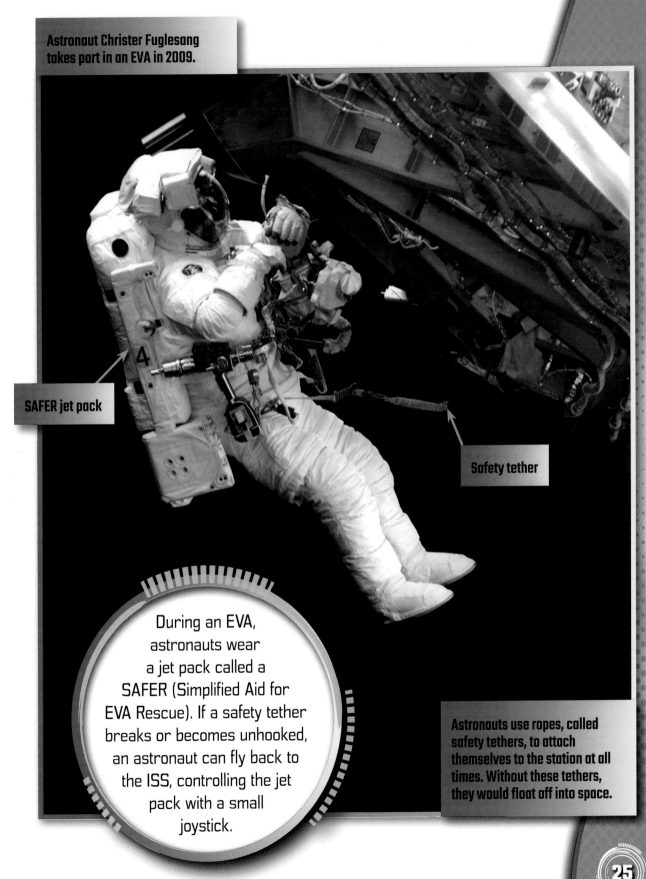

Astronaut Christer Fuglesang takes part in an EVA in 2009.

SAFER jet pack

Safety tether

During an EVA, astronauts wear a jet pack called a SAFER (Simplified Aid for EVA Rescue). If a safety tether breaks or becomes unhooked, an astronaut can fly back to the ISS, controlling the jet pack with a small joystick.

Astronauts use ropes, called safety tethers, to attach themselves to the station at all times. Without these tethers, they would float off into space.

The Journey Home

When a mission is over, the crew returns to Earth in their *Soyuz* spacecraft. The spacecraft undocks from the ISS and continues to orbit Earth. Then, about an hour before landing, the spacecraft makes a de-orbit burn. This slows it down and causes it to start falling back toward Earth.

At about 87 miles (140 km) above Earth's surface, the spacecraft separates into its three modules. Then, the tiny descent module containing the crew plunges into Earth's **atmosphere**, traveling at about 17,400 miles per hour (28,000 km/h).

Friction caused by air starts to slow the craft, and parachutes are deployed to reduce its speed. When it is about 5 miles (8 km) above Earth's surface, the craft's main parachute opens.

Scott Kelly (left), Sergey Volkov (center), and Mikhail Kornienko (right) are crammed into the *Soyuz* descent module—ready to go home!

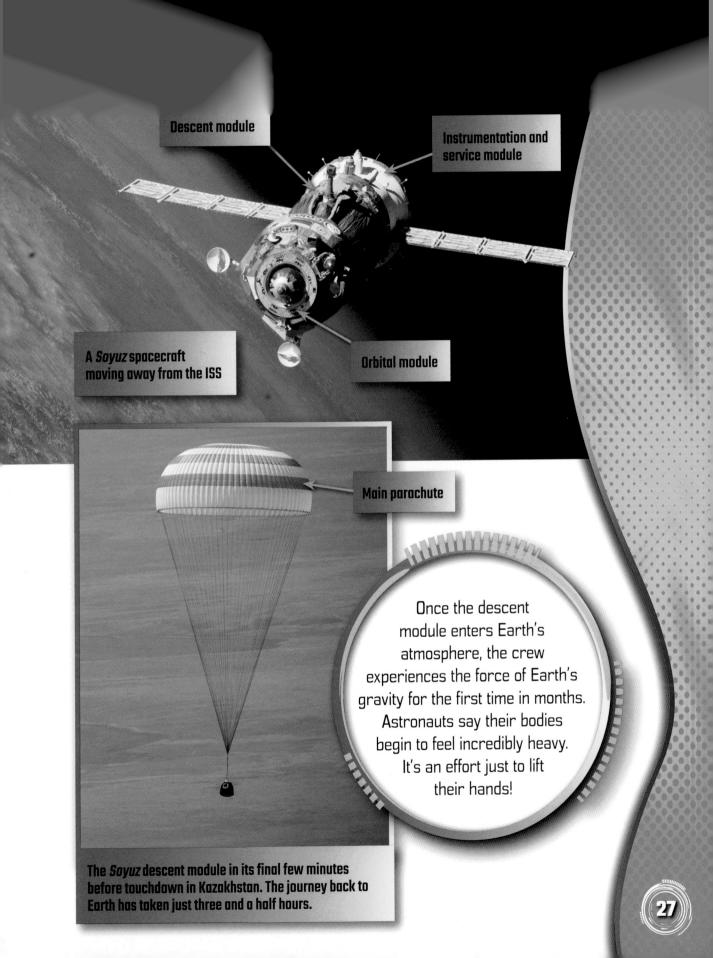

Descent module

Instrumentation and service module

A *Soyuz* spacecraft moving away from the ISS

Orbital module

Main parachute

Once the descent module enters Earth's atmosphere, the crew experiences the force of Earth's gravity for the first time in months. Astronauts say their bodies begin to feel incredibly heavy. It's an effort just to lift their hands!

The *Soyuz* descent module in its final few minutes before touchdown in Kazakhstan. The journey back to Earth has taken just three and a half hours.

Welcome Back to Earth

The descent module is slowed by its parachute and by firing six rockets. Then . . . Bang. It hits the ground—hard!

Medical and rescue crews rush to the descent module and help the astronauts from their spacecraft. For the first time in months, the crew enjoys the taste and smell of fresh air. The astronauts are overjoyed to be home and will soon be reunited with their families. Their bodies, however, will take many months, and possibly years, to recover from their long stay in space.

One day, space scientists hope to send astronauts to Mars and perhaps beyond. The human body experiments underway on the ISS today will help make this goal a reality. So will the **pioneering** men and women who go to work on the space station.

Astronauts describe the *Soyuz* touchdown as feeling like being in a small car in a head-on collision with an enormous truck!

Samantha Cristoforetti is helped from the *Soyuz* descent module by the rescue crew as her ISS mission ends on June 11, 2015.

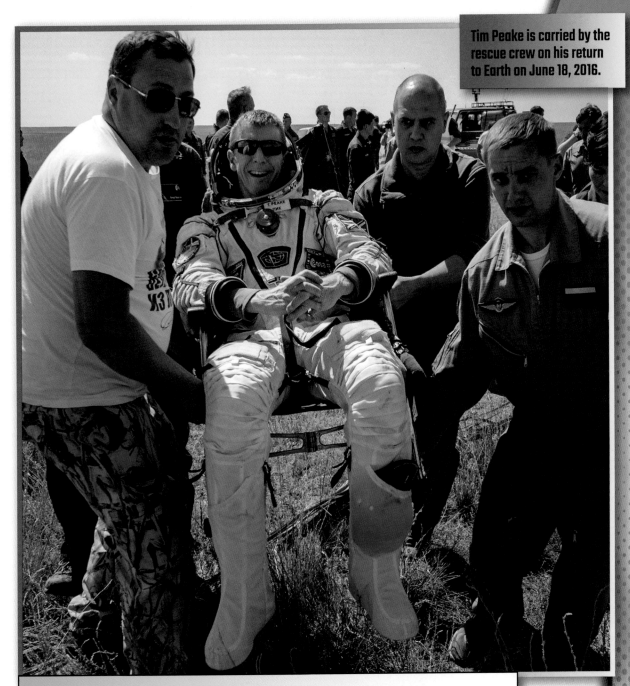

Tim Peake is carried by the rescue crew on his return to Earth on June 18, 2016.

The Human Body in Space

Astronauts have many physical problems to overcome when they return to Earth.

- They suffer EMS (Entry Motion Sickness), which causes headaches, dizziness, and vomiting.

- They may feel faint as the brain relearns the difference between up and down.

- The body feels heavy as gravity causes blood to flow from the upper body back to the lower body.

- Breathing can be difficult as the body adjusts to gravity.

- Speaking can feel strange as an astronaut's lips and tongue have gotten used to weightlessness.

- Skin feels highly sensitive—even rain can hurt.

- Bones have weakened and will break more easily.

- Muscles are weak due to weightlessness.

Get to Work as an Astronaut

What qualities are needed to be an astronaut?
- A high level of physical fitness, including excellent eyesight
- A head for heights
- Good mental health and stable personality—astronauts must spend long periods of time away from their families, in a dangerous, high-pressure, claustrophobic environment.
- High level of motivation
- Good concentration
- Good memory

What subjects should I study to become an astronaut?
At school, study math and science, including computer science. In college you will need a degree in math, biology, physics, medicine, engineering, or computer science.

Can pilots become astronauts?
Some astronaut candidates come from an aviation background. To be considered, a pilot has usually flown in the military and must have at least 1,000 hours of flying time.

What happens during the selection process?
Astronaut candidates will undergo extensive physical examinations. They also take hundreds of hours of exams to test their intelligence and other skills.

What are my chances?
Only a lucky few get to become astronauts. For every astronaut that goes into space, however, there is a team of thousands of scientists and engineers on the ground who make it happen. Good luck!

Design a Space Experiment

What experiment would you like to do on the ISS?

1. Begin by thinking about these questions and doing research.
What are the difficulties for humans aboard the ISS? How does weightlessness or experiencing 16 days and nights in every 24-hour period affect living things?

Your proposed experiment might include humans, animals, or plants. It could also investigate materials, water—the list is endless!

2. Plan your experiment.
- What is the science question you wish to ask and answer?
- Do background research.
- Construct a hypothesis.
- What experiment will you do in space to test the hypothesis? What equipment will you need? Is your experiment practical to take into space?

The word "astronaut" comes from the Greek words *astron* and *nautes*, which mean "star sailor."

What's in Your Space Suitcase?

An astronaut's clothes, washing equipment, and food are all supplied aboard the ISS. However, astronauts still like to take some personal belongings with them.

Each astronaut has a luggage allowance of just under 3 pounds (1.4 kg).

1. If you were going to the ISS for six months, what would you take?

2. Gather all the items and weigh them on kitchen scales. Can you stay within the luggage allowance?

Do you like learning languages? Aboard the ISS, the crew speaks English and Russian. All astronaut trainees must learn to speak both languages fluently.

Glossary

atmosphere (AT-muh-sfeer)
A layer of gases around a planet, moon, or star.

contaminate (kuhn-TAM-uh-nate)
To harm or make something unclean by introducing something dirty or dangerous.

cosmonaut (KOZ-muh-nawt)
A Russian astronaut.

data (DAY-tuh)
Information and facts, often in the form of numbers.

docked (DOKT)
Securely connected to a space station or spacecraft.

engineer (en-juh-NIHR)
A person who uses math, science, and technology to design, build, and repair machines or structures.

EVA (Extravehicular Activity)
(ek-struh-vee-HIK-yoo-lur ac-TIV-uh-tee)
A spacewalk made by astronauts outside of the ISS or a spacecraft.

gravity (GRA-vuh-tee)
The force that causes objects to be pulled toward other objects.

laboratory (LA-bruh-tor-ee)
A room, building, or vehicle where there is equipment that can be used to carry out experiments and other scientific studies.

orbit (OR-bit)
To circle, or move around, another object.

oxygen (OK-suh-juhn)
An invisible gas in air that people and animals need to breathe.

pioneering (pye-uh-NEER-ing)
The first to do something; leading the way.

radiation (ray-dee-AY-shun)
A type of invisible energy that travels through space. High levels of radiation can be harmful to living things.

simulator (SIM-yuh-lay-tur)
A pretend version of something, such as a plane, spacecraft, or building.

solar array (SOH-lur uh-RAY)
A group of solar panels joined together.

water molecule
(WAW-tur MOL-uh-kyool)
The smallest unit of water, formed from two hydrogen atoms and one oxygen atom attached to each other.

Index

Read More

Owen, Ruth.
Living on Mars (It's a Fact!).
New York: Ruby Tuesday Books (2015).

Riddolls, Tom.
Sally Ride: The First American Woman in Space (Crabtree Groundbreaker Biographies). New York: Crabtree Publishing Company (2010).

Learn More Online

To learn more about astronauts and life in space, go to:
www.rubytuesdaybooks.com/astronauts